Are We Not All *Mothers?*

SHERI DEW

DESERET BOOK
SALT LAKE CITY, UTAH

Sources Cited

Ballard, Melvin J. *Sermons and Missionary Services of Melvin Joseph Ballard.* Bryant S. Hinckley, comp. Salt Lake City: Deseret Book, 1949.

Clark, J. Reuben, Jr. "Our Wives and Our Mothers in the Eternal Plan." *Relief Society Magazine,* December 1946, 801.

Cowley, Matthew. *Matthew Cowley Speaks.* Salt Lake City: Deseret Book, 1954.

Hinckley, Gordon B. *Teachings of Gordon B. Hinckley.* Salt Lake City: Deseret Book, 1997.

———. "Walking in the Light of the Lord." *Ensign,* November 1998, 97–100.

Kimball, Spencer W. "The Role of Righteous Women." *Ensign,* November 1979, 102–4.

"The Message of the First Presidency to the Church." *Improvement Era,* November 1942, 761.

Packer, Boyd K. *The Things of the Soul.* Salt Lake City: Bookcraft, 1996.

Smith, Lucy Mack. *The History of Joseph Smith by His Mother.* Revised and enhanced edition. Scot Facer Proctor and Maurine Jensen Proctor, eds. Salt Lake City: Bookcraft, 1996.

Widtsoe, John A. *Priesthood and Church Government.* Salt Lake City: Deseret Book, 1939.

Visit us at DeseretBook.com

ISBN 978-1-60908-728-9

Printed in the United States of America
Artistic Printing, Salt Lake City, UT

10 9 8 7 6 5 4 3 2 1

One summer, four teenage nieces and I shared a tense Sunday evening when we set out walking from a downtown hotel in a large U.S. city where we were visiting to a nearby chapel where I had been invited to speak at a fireside. I had walked that exact route many times before, but that evening as we left our hotel we suddenly found ourselves engulfed by an enormous crowd of rowdy parade-goers who were streaming out of the city toward the suburbs. Though police were everywhere, it was obviously no place for four teenage girls—or for their aunt, for that matter. But with the streets closed to traffic, and therefore no cabs available, we had no choice but to keep walking. Feeling no small amount of anxiety, I turned toward the girls, gathered them around me, and shouted over the din, "Stay right with me. Don't take your eyes off me." With that, I began to maneuver my way through the crush of largely inebriated humanity, constantly looking behind me to make sure the girls were right there. A walk that should have taken forty-five minutes at most was taking much longer. But I quickly forgot the time, because the only thing on my mind was my nieces' safety. There were moments when I truly feared we would not make it to the church in one piece. Drunken men with boa constrictors draped around their necks and adolescents brandishing weapons sometimes blocked our way. It was intimidating, to say the least.

Though our walk ultimately took twice as long as it should have, we finally made it to the chapel. I can still remember the immense relief that rushed over me as we walked across the threshold into the church. But for ninety unnerving minutes, I better understood how mothers feel who forgo their own safety to protect their children. My siblings had entrusted me with their daughters, whom I dearly love, and I would have done just about anything to protect them and to lead them safely to our destination.

In similar fashion, our Father has entrusted us, His daughters, with His children, and He has asked us not only to love them but to help lead them safely through the crush of mortal humanity and past the dangers of this world back home.

Loving and *leading*—these words summarize not only the all-consuming work of the Father and the Son, but the essence of the labor of women, for the work of latter-day women of God is to help the Lord with His work. How, then, may latter-day women of God best help the Lord with His work?

Prophets have repeatedly answered this question, as did the First Presidency six decades ago, when they called motherhood "the highest, holiest service . . . assumed by mankind" ("Message of the First Presidency to the Church," 761).

Have you ever wondered why prophets have taught the doctrine of motherhood—*and it is doctrine*—again and again, and without even the slightest variation? I have. I have thought long and hard about the work of women of God. And I have wrestled with what the doctrine of motherhood means to all women. Because my life has unfolded in a manner far different from what I have hoped or expected or pleaded for, the issue of motherhood has driven me to my knees, to the scriptures, to the temple, and to the teachings of prophets, seers, and revelators—all of which teach an ennobling doctrine regarding the most crucial role any woman can be asked or allowed to assume. It is a doctrine about which we must be clear if we hope to stand "steadfast and immovable" (Mosiah 5:15)

Our Father has entrusted us, His daughters, with His children, and He has asked us not only to love them but to help lead them safely past the dangers of this world back home.

and unflinching regarding the issues that swirl around the female gender.

For Satan has declared war on motherhood and on the family. He does everything he can to dishonor and devalue both womanhood and motherhood. This fact is more apparent with every passing day. He well knows that those who rock the cradle are perhaps in the best possible position to rock his diabolical earthly empire. He knows that none of us could progress without receiving bodies and experiencing our second estate. He understands that without mothers who are willing to bear children, our Father's plan would be completely frustrated. He knows that without righteous mothers loving and leading the rising generation, the kingdom of God will fail.

If motherhood is divine and eternal and core to the nature of every woman—and it is—no wonder, then, that Lucifer would do everything in his considerable power to demean and undermine everything about motherhood, hoping to confuse women with worldly enticements or secular philosophies that appear more satisfying or dazzling or even more enlightening.

When we understand the magnitude of motherhood, it becomes clear why prophets have been so protective of woman's most sacred and divinely appointed role. While we tend to equate motherhood solely with maternity and to, in effect, limit it to that definition, in the Lord's language the word *mother* has layers of meaning. Of all the words or titles they could have chosen to define her role and her essence, both God the Father and Adam called Eve "the mother of all living" (Moses

4:26)—and they did so before she ever bore a child. "And Adam called his wife's name Eve, because she was the mother of all living; for thus have I, the Lord God, called the first of all women, which are many" (Moses 4:26).

The Lord does nothing with a short-range view. Everything He does is for forever. Thus, like Eve, our motherhood began before we were born. Just as worthy men were foreordained to hold the priesthood in mortality (see Alma 13:2–4, 7–8), righteous women were endowed premortally with the privilege and responsibility of motherhood. President Spencer W. Kimball taught that the assignments of men and women differ, "with women being given many tremendous responsibilities of motherhood and sisterhood and men being given the tremendous responsibilities of fatherhood and the priesthood—but the man is not without the woman nor the woman without the man in the Lord (see 1 Cor. 11:11)" ("Role of Righteous Women," 102). Motherhood is more than bearing children, though it is certainly and definitely that. It is the essence of who we are as women. Motherhood defines our very identity, our divine stature and nature, and the unique traits, talents, and tendencies with which our Father endowed us.

President Gordon B. Hinckley stated that "God planted within women something divine" (*Teachings of Gordon B. Hinckley*, 387). That something is the gift of and the gifts associated with motherhood. Elder Matthew Cowley of the Quorum of the Twelve taught that "men have to have something given to them [in mortality] to make them saviors of men, but not mothers, not women. [They] are born with an inherent right, an inherent authority, to be the saviors of human souls . . . and the regenerating force in the lives of God's children" (*Matthew Cowley Speaks,* 109).

Motherhood is not what was left over after our Father blessed His sons with the privilege of priesthood ordination. It was the most ennobling endowment He could give His daughters, a sacred trust that gave woman an unparalleled role in helping His children keep their second estate. As President J. Reuben Clark, Jr., declared, motherhood is "as divinely called, as eternally important in its place as the Priesthood itself" ("Our Wives and Our Mothers in the Eternal Plan," 801). And President Boyd K. Packer taught this: "The obligations of motherhood are never-ending. The addition of such duties as those which attend ordination to the priesthood would constitute an intrusion into, an interruption to, perhaps the avoidance of, that crucial contribution which only a mother can provide. The limitation of priesthood responsibilities to men is a tribute to the incomparable place of women in the plan of salvation. . . . Men and women have complementary, not competing, responsibilities. There is difference but not inequity. . . . In the woman's part, she is not equal to man; she is superior! She can do that which he can never do; not in all eternity can he do it" (*Things of the Soul,* 172).

No wonder President Gordon B. Hinckley declared that "mothers can do more than any other group" to reverse today's sobering social trends ("Walking in the Light of the Lord," 100).

There can be no question about how our Father feels about His daughters, whom He has charged with the principal care of His children. And there can be no question about why prophets ancient and modern have depended so heavily upon the influence of mothers, both in and outside the home, to help build the gospel kingdom.

Nevertheless, at times and in some circumstances, the words *mother* and *motherhood* have divided rather than united us. For the subject of motherhood is a very tender one, as it evokes some of our greatest joys and heartaches. This has been so from the very beginning. Eve was "glad" after the Fall, realizing she otherwise "never should have had seed" (Moses 5:11). And yet, imagine her anguish, sorrow, and suffering over Cain and her heartache about Abel. Some mothers experience pain because of the children they have borne; others feel pain because they do not have the privilege of bearing children here in mortality. About this Elder John A. Widtsoe was explicit: "Women who through no fault of their own cannot exercise the gift of motherhood directly, may do so vicariously" (*Priesthood and Church Government*, 85). And Elder Melvin J. Ballard stated, "God bless those mothers who are not yet permitted through no fault of their own to be mothers in very deed, but who are nevertheless mothers at heart" (*Sermons and Missionary Services of Melvin Joseph Ballard*, 206–7).

For reasons known to the Lord, some women are required to wait to have children. This delay and disappointment is not easy for any righteous woman. But the Lord's timetable for each of us does not negate or somehow change or cancel out our very nature. Some of us, then, must simply find other ways to mother. And all around us are those who need to be loved and led, nurtured and mentored. In other words, the spiritual rewards of mothering are available to all.

Eve set the pattern. In addition to bearing children, she mothered all of mankind when she made the most courageous decision any woman has ever made and with Adam opened the way for us to progress. She set an example of womanhood for men to respect and women to follow, modeling the characteristics with which we as women have been endowed: heroic faith, a keen sensitivity to the Spirit, an abhorrence of evil, and complete selflessness. Like the Savior, "who for the joy that was set before him endured the cross" (Hebrews 12:2), Eve, for the joy of helping initiate the human family, endured the Fall. She loved us enough to help lead us.

All around us are those who need to be loved and led, nurtured and mentored. The spiritual rewards of mothering are available to all.

As daughters of our Heavenly Father, and as daughters of Eve, we are all mothers and we have always been mothers. And we each have the responsibility and the privilege to love and to help lead the rising generation. How will our young women learn to live as women of God unless they see what women of God look like—meaning what we wear, watch, and read; how we fill our time and our minds; how we face temptation and uncertainty; where we find true joy; and why modesty and femininity are hallmarks of righteous women? How will our young men, on the other hand, learn to value women of God if we don't show them the virtue of our virtues? If we don't show them what kind of women will help them find the greatest joy and fulfillment in their lives, who will? One of the single most significant responsibilities for a latter-day woman of God—regardless of her personal circumstances—is to help love and lead the younger generation. If we don't mentor them, no one will. If we don't show them there is joy in living as followers of Christ, where else can they possibly expect to see it!

Every one of us has an overarching obligation to model righteous womanhood because our youth may not see it modeled anywhere else. Every sister in Relief Society, which is simply the most significant community of women on this side of the veil, is responsible to help our young women make a joyful transition into Relief Society. This means that our friendship with our young women must begin long before they turn eighteen. Every woman of God, regardless of our individual circumstances, can mother someone—beginning of course with the children in our own homes and families, but extending far beyond. Every woman of God can show by word and by deed that the work of women in the Lord's kingdom is magnificent and holy. How far will we go to rescue a child or rally a teenager to righteousness?

For when we save a young man or a young woman, we may save generations. I repeat: Every woman of God is a mother in Israel, and our calling is to help love and help lead the rising generation through the dangerous streets of mortality.

Few of us will reach our potential without the nurturing of both the mother who bore us and the mothers who bear with us. I was thrilled not long ago to see one of my youth leaders for the first time in years. As a teenager who had absolutely no self-confidence, I always sidled up to this woman because she would inevitably put her arm around me and say, "You are just the best girl!" She showed that she loved me, so I was willing to let her lead me. How many young men and women are desperate for your love and leadership and for your vote of confidence in them? Do we fully realize that our influence as mothers in Israel is irreplaceable and eternal?

When I was growing up, it was not uncommon for Mother to wake me in the middle of the night and say, "Sheri, take your pillow and go downstairs." I knew what that meant. We lived in Kansas, tornado country, and her words meant one of those deadly twisters was coming. My immediate reaction was always fear. But then Mom would inevitably say, "Sheri, everything will be okay." Her words always calmed me, and even as a child I instinctively sensed that my mother was constantly looking out for me.

Later, as I grew older and began to enter musical competitions or participate on athletic teams, before big games or performances, again, I would listen for my mother to say something like, "You can do it. You'll be great."

It is interesting that today, decades later, when life seems particularly overwhelming or frightening or just downright scary, I call Mother and listen for her to say, "Sheri, you can do it." A mother's influence not only spans decades, it reaches into the eternities.

There are few women who exemplify this better than Lucy Mack Smith, mother of the Prophet Joseph. Long before her son had the experience in the Sacred Grove that commenced the Restoration, she was seeking to find the original gospel preached by the Savior as recorded in the scriptures. She went to one meeting with high hopes and recorded: "I went in expectation of obtaining that which alone could satisfy my soul—the bread of eternal life. When the minister commenced, I fixed my mind with breathless attention upon the spirit and matter of the discourse, but all was emptiness, vanity, vexation of spirit, and fell upon my heart like the chill, untimely blast upon the starting ear ripening in a summer sun. . . . I was almost in total despair, and with a grieved and troubled spirit I returned home, saying in my heart, there is not on earth the religion which I seek. I must again turn to my Bible, take Jesus and his disciples for an example."

When she nearly died of tuberculosis, she wrote, "I covenanted with God that if he would let me live, I would endeavor to get that religion that would enable me to serve him right, whether it was in the Bible or wherever it might be found, even if it was to be obtained from heaven by prayer and faith" (*History of Joseph Smith by His Mother,* 48–50).

Surely Lucy Mack's fundamental faith, searching, and

spiritual sensitivity paved the way for all that would happen to her sons Joseph and Hyrum. Her influence has clearly reached into the eternities.

After the horrifying events of September 11, 2001, U.S. First Lady Laura Bush was asked to recount what she did during those initial minutes after she heard about the terrorist attack. "I called my children immediately to reassure them," she said, adding, "and then I called my own mother, just for the comfort of her voice" ("Laura Bush, Comforter in Chief," from WashingtonPost.com, 21 September 2001).

Terrorist activities and ongoing armed conflicts underscore the fact that we live in a world of uncertainty and unmitigated evil. Never has there been a greater need for righteous mothers—mothers who bless their children with a sense of security and confidence about the future, mothers who teach that the only place they will find peace, truth, and enduring safety is in Jesus Christ, for His power is always stronger than the power of the adversary.

Recently one of my sisters found an old notebook containing the minutes of a home Primary our mother held in 1957 because there was only one Primary-age child in our little branch—a four-year-old girl. Me. Week after week, Mother prepared a lesson and taught a song. Usually there was one visitor: my two-year-old brother. Page after page records the consistent efforts of a young mother to teach her children the gospel.

That notebook has caused me to reflect yet again on the

countless ways Mother helped set the course for my life. For what a mother teaches a child doesn't get erased.

Every time we build the faith or reinforce the nobility of a young woman or man, every time we love or lead anyone even one small step along the path, we are true to our endowment and calling and inherent nature as mothers. No woman who understands the gospel would ever think that any other work is more important or would ever say, "I am just a mother," for mothers heal the souls of men.

I invite every woman to look around. Who needs you and your influence? Who needs your healing, nurturing touch? Who needs someone to understand them and to believe in them? Who needs to hear you say, "I know things are going to be all right," or, "You can do it. I know you can."

If we really want to make a difference, it will happen as we mother those we have borne and those we are willing to bear with. If we will stay right with our youth—meaning, if we will love them—in most cases, they will stay right with us, meaning, they will let us lead them. And in the process we will find joy, for as Elder John A. Widtsoe declared, "Where women choose to magnify their motherhood, either direct or vicarious, progress and happiness is the sure result" (*Priesthood and Church Government,* 90).

As mothers in Israel, we *are* the Lord's secret weapon. Our influence comes from a divine endowment that has been in place from the beginning. In the premortal world, when our Father described our role, I wonder if we didn't stand in wide-eyed wonder that He would bless us with a sacred trust so central to His plan and that He would endow us with gifts so vital to the loving and leading of His children. I wonder if we shouted for joy (see Job 38:7) at least in part because of the ennobling stature He gave us in His kingdom. The world won't tell you that, but the Spirit will.

> *Mothers heal the souls of men.*

We just cannot let the Lord down. And if the day comes when Latter-day Saint women are the only women on earth who find nobility and divinity in motherhood, so be it. For *mother* is the word that will define a righteous woman made perfect in the highest degree of the celestial kingdom, a woman who has qualified for eternal increase in posterity, wisdom, joy, and influence.

These doctrines about the divine role of women are true, and when understood they bring peace and purpose to all women. The challenge of all latter-day women of God is to rise to the responsibility of being mothers in these perilous times, though doing so may test the last ounce of our endurance and courage and faith. Our challenge is to stand steadfast and immovable and unflinching as mothers in Israel and women of God. Our Father and His Only Begotten Son have given us a sacred stewardship and a holy crown in Their kingdom. May we rejoice in it. And may we be worthy of Their trust.